MATERIAL GIRL

Laura Jaramillo

subpress 2012

Many thanks to Angela Ostaudelafont Romano and Joseph Romano, Mary Hoeffel, Steve Dolph, Ryan Eckes, Michael Nicoloff, Claire Sandberg-Bernard, Magdalena Zurawski, Daniel Lin, Luis Fernando Jaramillo, Eileen Myles, David Need (and the participants of the Reading Circle), Adra Raine, Marta Villota, María Salgado, Christine Hou, and Lucia Ostaudelafont.

Also, many thanks to the editors of *The Recluse*, *The Poker*, Elective Affinities, and Contrabando, in which portions of this book have appeared.

Subpress Books are distributed by Small Press Distribution, www.spdbooks.org

Cover Image by Marta Villota
Design and Typesetting by The Mass Ornament

Contents

it's the opaque desire to communicate
of a landscape in flames

-ready

The Reactionary Poems

IT'S MORNING IN AMERICA

The central hypocrisies are obscured
in that
Language is beautiful
in the distant crackle of pre-
recorded applause
in the ululations that are
certitude and color.

TROPICAL FASCISM

Writing is boring
and difficult today I am full

of stupid jealousies even the ad
copy and gossip rags

'holiday trips to a country
at war' are lines from

a half-finished war
poem births that uncomfortable

sensation, having been
only a proxy for myself

F U U THINK YOU ARE THE GOD
OF PAINTBALL

I spend too much
time convincing
myself the language
belongs as
much to me
as it does
to them. I am still
not convinced

POST-HEROIC DRAG

How could the word 'post-
heroic' even
exist but it does
exist–imported
not from advertising
but from theories
invented to sell
concepts in the *field*
of advertising.

POST-HEROIC DRAG pt. II

Still, she drags her tired
arches her five o'clock
shadow her leathery
bosom into the empty
street

THE WOODY ALLENIZATION
OF THE SPECIES

Before bed, potential structures:
rooms that open onto gardens
gardens onto peonies or paper
whites O'Hara's
poems Homer's blind
swept brine
ness blazing
in speech and
in carriage. Deliver me with an arrow
in the tendon/a small storm
in the frontal lobe
to sleep to dreams
tedious
as living

IF YOU DON'T COME TO THE
PLANTAIN GROVE I'LL DIE

You and I keep a box
of shit and pissy
sediment in the kitchen

PSYCHIC DUGOUT

Go there
so our eyes can't
meet here
across the room the Yankees
are playing
like shit this year

HAWAIIAN PUNCH BLACK OUT

It's the kind of party? that's like
a wake too, you know?

Yes, we're made ghosts
kids show up

continue becoming:
apparition
libation.

EROS HOSIERY CO.

Eating this ham sandwich
other transhuman
activities may cross my mind

some endlessly
rehearsed difficulties
in the pregnant heat
like breathing and fucking

TECHNOLOGY PLUS THE ABSENCE
OF LOVE

The morass, aging super-
models, mid-90's danceable
soft rap and wading
            through this–
Who'll be the dirty
agonist in the future face
an oval Buddha to escape
the rain in a corporate
arcade

WHAT THERE IS TO SAY ABOUT REALITY
THAT HAS NOT ALREADY BEEN SAID

Amidst these trees I've invented
and which are not trees
I stand.

                    -Roberto Bolaño

It's totally not that much
like art.

EPIC MINIMALISM

I, on the other hand, am
miniaturizing so my anger
doesn't lose its
scale.

ABSTRACT REALISM

The Arts & Leisure section informs
you it's time to aspire to
rather than flee
solitude—
authentic but
stylized.

TRANSCENDENTAL IRONY

The church next door
has no sense of music
yet it's the meat
of their communion
with God.

The tambourines'
harangue through
pasteboard—
the very
music
of humanity.

FWD: WE ARE THE PROTAGONISTS AND ARCHITECTS OF OUR OWN DESTINY!

Time is an autoclave spinning
Or time
Is a clavichord played by a nun
eternally it's Tuesday
again. The manuscript is incomplete
on the table the starlings x out the
name of Fate in their restless criss
crossing. Stack of words, Present
and future are false
antinomies

MORTGAGES FOR ALL CREDIT SCENARIOS

I miss Philly like I miss
my father which is how
I can tell the wound
dimensions
not to say–
my father's dead
      neither is Philly

but that from
the wound pours light
on the fact of being
flesh in the world

I live here now.
Who'll return New
York City to its humanity

17

UNREAL ESTATE

"Sometimes I arrive here and I am standing
outside Law and Government High
School"-man waiting to get into Bronx Family Court

a unit of measurement that
means: several hundred yards
away

WITHOUT ROOF OR LAW

Nationalism is when
all the women wear the colors
of the flag on their person/dress
the argument that every
thing smaller
than the nation itself ought
to be dwarfed by the flag

The movie was distributed
in the Americas
under the title *Vagabond*
a value judgment
rather than a translation. The girl
I mean–, the one in the movie–
was a speck in the eye
of the nation, the tilled wild-
erness.

PEACE CEREAL FOR BREAKFAST

National Public Radio says we dream it so
it's on t.v. and dreaming is:

We are lovely
today large and violent
as a Trojan horse
insurgent
waves crest
against our copper
belly and we believe
all atoms are agents
in our war.

ÁCA YA NO ME DESVELO

Caught insomnia from *Cops*
lifted from sleep to the bosom of the Law
with firecrackers or

gunfire I think of Absolute Pacifism and the
history of ideas is longer than the future

YOUNG AMERICANS MASSACRED BY ILLEGAL ALIENS

The autopsy report
on Science
Fiction revealed
prose all purple
inside the belly and
Today inside its maw

BORICUA MOTORS

Sitting on the hood
of a fancy car in a parking
lot in New
Jersey there's a sense of
getting over

The air is gray
green you've got that half-
immigrant
pallor

YOU COULDA GOT SHOT, SAL

The teenagers are gathered at
the corner of 11th and
Wolf in front of the church
to guard the sieve
through which all black
people in the world
enter

I LIKE VIOLENCE CUZ THEY SMELL NICE

They buried the books

In the careless soil
overlooking a stream

Beyond, a man throws
tallboys at a possum.

Civilian Nest

AS SAFE AND WARM AS A POODLE
IN ITS OWNER'S LAP

In the other room, the girls are
laughing over a received tone
of high tragedy

Your mom called:
and your childhood?

   —it doesn't remember you. In fact, you induce amnesia
in everyone you meet when the movie drifts into
Dream t.v. slip into over-
the-counter sleep with John Cleese
denatured rhythms rise
to meet the dark each day

p.s. Every
building where your limbs
lengthened has been
razed

CONNECTICUT ROCOCO

My heart is a cat wearing a Hello
Kitty costume, the dumb immutable self dressed up as a version
and you, like a hologram vanishing and shining there sometimes the
t.v. with its moon face casting rays days like Thursday, I am too dim in
my own being
to be present.

A half-moon is a cut-out in shutters
that cut off the house from the station wagon's
lights pushing a path through the pines. A sign on the highway
reads, If you lived here,

you'd already be home, a statement etched in perceptual
error.

       Q: Are you home tonight?

       A: No.

Instead, it's absolute darkness early
in the corn chandeliers, in the apple trees that are
bear pantries blue viscous evening where you are
for a while
until I return myself to myself. Forty percent of anxiety
sufferers report seeing

ghosts and blood pouring beneath doors.
Negative ecstasy. Horror is the marrow
of work
and loving, sometimes too.

MUSIC FOR BLOWN OUT SPEAKERS

"I am a man who loves beauty" but good design
    levels difference,
    knows no pluralities
    that can't be halved
    and quartered. As if poetic diction,
as if that supremely
      impersonal avant-garde could pave over, even express
            our peasant sufferings

                Eye ehma men of constant sorroh
                aye seen trouble all meh days

The electric bill is a paper wing entering that familiar inferno, it's December
ninth the economic life of the polis is slipping my father says this is the end
of the neoliberal myth the bits from which it's woven: newsprint mylar
bendy straws falling away faster than anybody The problem with Marxist-
Leninists is they ask you
                constantly
                to make films for the revolution.

Handbag vendors nested in a retrospective of Takashi Murakami
artisan-made flowers and smiley faces great streams of jism
from the cock of a cartoon

thousands of janus-faced spheres one side
is winsome the other is
cruel but,

MR. MURAKAMI, DEATH IS NO SHRINKY DINK. Let me warn you:
The mask of strangeness

always falls off the face of convention.

Plastic articulated as

plastic.

SLOBODAN MILOSEVIC IS NOT A WAR CRIMINAL

The neighborhood is full of these posters
someone says sort of an uphill political rehabilitation
    huh? someone says credit or
      debit?
      Danjiela disagrees, He is a national hero rings up the frozen
                pizza young women's infinite seriousness
                holds up the nation state even after there's
                no nation
      and no state.

Her notebook
says on its cover
Danjiela plus Miguelito
made in Jugoslavijia/
Hecho en Mexico.

        Someone says into their celly
           I'm mean, but I'm humble.

Vishnu the fish
monger says I don't eat
meat
I don't treat

my body
like a graveyard I pray
and fast
read the Holy Bible when I feel
Hunger I pray
more an ounce of pink and blue translucent skeleton
per pound of de-veined shrimp. Overfished striped bass
tuna and fluke, the age of Pisces coming
to a close. Your
earthly lot
a bloodied
shin compared to
this your faith
polite shiv
in my agnostic face

TRAMPOLINE THE STRANGER

Here an old woman adjusts scarves around her
  wrinkles in a small pink hand
mirror around her kids pretend to gun each
other down. In a neighborhood otherwise known as Greece,
Doric columns/firs
and Aristotle thinking
   Somewhere the sun is rising over a city we have not yet known
   somewhere someone is writing the history of punk in Bucharest
   this
 the inexplicable root of all solitude
    has its tentacles round the foundations
    to sense but never know home
      is a public
      works project this park was given to the
      city of New York by Mayor Rudolph W.
Giuliani, our horned/fanged household
deity. A city is structure and admixture never
exactly what one would have it be.
      One lays down in protest.
is prone and dangerous, illness and
dreams, accumulated intimacies spill
on pavement unlaundered sheets
trampoline the stranger

into an unknown

unwanted psyche. It's May

and NOT OK to make your bed in public? The subway grates

traditionally layered with cloth blankets rags sleeping

bags plastic tarps that trap heat for indigents in winter get

covered with upright benches

atop brushed steel waves

fitted with sharp ridges

along the length of Steinway Street

IO NO HO VOTATO PER BERLUSCONI

Well, we (poets)
have a code which I can tell you
now that the jig is up. We place
the (commemorative) Reagan stamps
upside down on
the envelopes, then we abdicate
the very idea
of communication

GROW AND BULLET-PROOF YOUR MONEY

A naked schizophrenic climbs out his apartment window
onto a bodega awning, waves a long fluorescent
light bulb like a

       light saber at the cops below, who tase him. He falls head
first to his death the footage blurs out
his genitals. Protect me from the wrong obscenity, evening news,

       Send Problem Solvers to tax payers.
A man in a matte black wig to investigate that ding
in her credit score

       not mine—abiding, but avoidant of the Law
in addition, he recommends:
Got no money?
That's no reason not to go
admire the fruits of capital, lacquered
gleaming in their cases
the best ones, food-like, but not

    food at least the department store knows its place as a space of
    commerce the mall shits where it eats the cats shit only when we come
    home the nest is built from spit VHS spools fur the crumpled
    duvet fine veils of dust books form the minaret

       Babel/Accumulation
       is the lust
       syllables, objects

have for coming into
Being.
In the lackluster city,
people live crammed in cubbies full
of nothing or full of mess.

Smoking on a fire escape she
tells me she would *gladly*
amputate a limb, euthanize her
pets to stay here
on this island. What
could be more valuable than TOTAL
MOBILITY through an URBAN LANDSCAPE?

THE CULTURE THE UNIVERSITY?
Q: What's been bothering you?
A: This place that can't keep its place -ness to itself

THE SUBLIME IS NOW

Dear Aunt Lucia, I don't doubt aliens
exist but I can't believe in aliens. The
rose of apocalypse so perfumed with danger
darkens the pavement passes in front of the moon
and the phone card is out
of minutes
Everybody
is becoming
      who they truly are
not sun gods

SUBURBIA/SOBERBIA

The town tonight
is inexpressive full
of secrets—related mostly to raw hatred but on its face
listless. The shrubs are so stark

        standing there
        outside the pharmacy
        not folded neatly into other phenomena

like water and grass. The actors in the herbicide ad
swear they couldn't look their neighbors in the eye
due to the dandelions
dotting the front lawn
wispy seeds on a high wire act
across the afternoon light
little suns exploding
everywhere.

An Ecuadorian man is stabbed to death in Patchogue by seven teenagers
on the hunt for "Mexicans" election night, November 4th in Franklin Square
my Colombian mother in her dark den takes pictures of the t.v.
my stepfather gone to bed. Along the island's length her
isolation in sharp relief shimmers on our cold collective tears.

        Q: Can utopia contain us all?

The house across the street

its vinyl siding applied

vertically

and

horizontally

is identified as a gross violation

a blatant concentration of evil eye

in the universe around which

all events whirl and the neighbors can't

control it, don't understand her when

she talks, not the content

the accent. She says

Nothing is ever complete

has her garden. Many hatreds unfurl against the flowering of that

uncertain intonation.

        She drives around for hours we drink
        expired Diet Coke it tastes like ghosts

SUMMER OF DEATH

R.I.P.
Pina Bausch
David Carradine
Farrah Fawcett
Michael Jackson
Garrick Holmquest
Merce Cunningham
Walter Cronkite
Tom Bernard
Dash Snow
John Hughes

And now it's high-tide
inside me crossing Park
today the site of untold
nihilism full of taxis,
tulips the yellows
mingle I turn away
from art/union/the
family—arguably,
we have none
of these but
—fog

over the city

a sunny haze

with ambulances

we're disconnected all this

ringing

      brutality

inside

          The tulips on Park Avenue die are replaced three

          times each summer sacerdotal white caps on fuschia

          robes whether there is no rain or too much rain

              shielded from vulgarity,

              advertising

              time by their petals the insurance

        of the rich

is not that they're exempt from tragedy,

exactly—it's that they're

insulated from lack

of beauty. The Armory

housing contemporary

art and war tanks beneath its floor the Upper

East Side tended like a country graveyard

stands squat and regal women wander panty-

hosed with their solitude in fur coats

lost

you're allowed to

walk through because
someone you know is
buried
here

> cars would pull over to the side of the road to let country
> funeral processions pass but today *people have no respect* a cousin
> of yours quips this day in Indiana smells deeply of rain
> bottomless, abstract as waxy flowers
> flanked around the basement

I forgot to say earlier
my heart looks more
like a Black Flag tattoo
> ill-advised but telling—
capable of Protestant feats
of abnegation. Old-fashioned
to not act selfish but my martyr
complex wears opera gloves to
fly/penetrate deeper into the heart
of your subjectivity folly
to be bound and rent by darkness
riding bareback through
the living room. Love, I'm moved
by frailty
ugliness

Your long pointy feet their bone spurs blades of calcium
peak beneath bluish skin. They cut me in the night and my
empathy borders on masochism. Love, you make sad feelings
into material history, this year others

        dying and us

        left

        living, few other artifacts

        just this fact

        the joints hum

hot and burn pressed to the chest
barks this is no thing and truly,
it's no thing to cover vast ground by Greyhound to
funerals. There are two women in nightgowns who'd like
to use your cell phone in the Art
Deco Cleveland bus station flanked by some high modern
ironies—man refuses
to be perfected, even improved
by architecture

BOHEMIA LIES BY THE SEA

Woman on the train middle-
school teacher mien complains
      her apartment near the Mister Softee depot
Tuesdays hosed down trucks
ice cream runs thick
on the curb grimes the gutters. Sugar
covers shoes skin
hair dull sheen of
dairy fuzzes streets,
says I'm learning to live with
      filth milky *Bohemia...*
at the Met
      —tire tracks cut a path through sweet pink wildflowers—
      Black horizon. Maybe an ocean
      or nothing lies
      in the distance
    haze hanging on ambivalence, landscape
      From the N, you see a
      Northern Blvd building super
      hanging
      a painting
      some pastoral sky on the roof,

                    Loop
                    a hook
                    onto the chain
                    link fence

The title's a wink it takes
years to get: Bohemia's not
by the sea at all, might not
even exist but he
cracks this joke at me we
haven't laughed in days
                    Q: Are we friends?
                    A: When we're friends I'm
Naples lift the Catholic
smog from our
pagan
secrets, split
the lip of retail power
couples
rend the terror
of Mondays,
excise sentimentality / replace
with pure love. Pork is roasted and dope is smoked freely
                    uplifted to outlaws by the general

lawlessness, at once inured to violence

and glad, slightly out of its reach,

raw nerves of each to each

under drop ceilings.

Nervous dogs howl inside a tight distance the doll

house/row home trembles with

hallucinatory joy music

fills the street an ice cream truck's

fenders scrape curb

warm breeze collapses inside

outside the light

cuts corneas in

mid-summer night

murk gasoline mingled

with milk.

Talk to me collapse

inside and out

friend/

mirage

milk-dense

noise the ice cream truck's just

in the other room

Material Girl

MATERIAL GIRL

Painters argue vehemently against this
that blue doesn't exist without
its word

where we
take it as an article of faith I still believe

in current events, language,
morning, civic languor the weather's

pigment as important as anything we talk about it
non-stop

    —it's cerulean
or its non-
sky color

Matter in the symbolic universe

of a day magazines pile
in the ante-

room of the shrink's office an editorial
states it would take no less

than a revolution in the structure
of family
to bring about true feminism

But the ladies,
they have so many choices now
they wear high heels they wear sneakers

on the way to work the hours empty themselves

in the humid subway
cheap chocolate
blooms from age in its wrapper

on the newsstand
through a series
of sound-proof

doors our mutual/objective/interlocutor
helps the women

their broken
intimacies shared/in shards

splayed through that white noise
machine's hiss

She brings her lunch in
a Victoria's Secret bag
pink for the shrink's receptionist
rudeness is a religion

today, she's cheerful wearing a sweater
with a rhinestone noose

bedazzled on the shoulder
she's nothing

if not the guardian
of my sleep where
she says start recycling

your mental pornography
your fantasy life is dying

But I'm awake

in the thick
of our newly-affirmed liberal

democracy, a feeling of not
feeling the Spring

but its linden trees:
an essence of Clorox and semen

flowering that doubles as the new
year aging lots of books disappear

in the move flip-flops get left
behind in a trash bag
I get here and have no house

shoes, don't know where
to buy milk a thirst awake in the cold

morning the years get written

on the backs of pharmacy receipts:

cat food trash bags sort movies/books
clean bathroom pack papers burn sage

sweet grass

non-epic accretion
of happenings: attachment ending

absence
crowding out night silence

Noise, not unlike
music

from another time
invades the room

gather up the animals they call it companionate love

here without
the fiction that I is anyone

but I the receptionist

or the imaginary 'before'
of this building

taking calls from black sand the city
beneath us collects downward towards

infinity taking calls belies

today's artificiality the internet doubles as

sleep talking and talking

as if Manhattan still existed

●

The immigrant mothers of America
do not approve this message

or the use of psycho-
tropics

in the treatment of depression it's their party
line netting chores across dawn

rescued from a scrubbing
global
under-class gratitude

in order
but the offspring
go off, join

the international drifting
class owners of stars and flowers,

or at least, the idea of them
structures mapped onto

the real sky the real earth militate against this order / the idea

of the subway
persists strongly

in the dream mind ideas
of the mother

persists in a prone body you

will ride beside me many nights and years

inscribing order
into palms

circa 1981 tokens
a keyhole

cut through the center
to view the invading blue

of a snowy twilit planet in March

western Queens massed together tight
and damp industrial garbage by the rails

violent neon filigree
graffiti

Veil them in names and dates graffiti veil us in names

and dates square ancient windows

Snoopy getting dusted

wakeful inside physical

sleep ride in an eyelet
lace communion

dress rabbit fur-trimmed
tiara cross-town

ride with a purse obtained in
'85 on sale at Alexander's your coat

swaddling my shoulders dove gray
wings crown the bridge supports

sully the pavement

(to swaddle: a Catholic verb)

on a 7:30 express mothers
its

children's eyes
weighted with morning
drift deep

from the el into rough
black basalt

their dreams are their own flecked with melting snow

physical dust / my labor must exist

•

Five o'clock's gone again

return marks the months
hurtling into anti-

Odyssey to never reach home
tonight the blue eternal lyric

you'll be there accusing me the bestiary
catalogue of blisters

the bright and multifarious heels of women

click dislocated in space
and time echoing around inside me

black and white marble chess board tiles

breaking the inviolate elegance of the Bloomingdale's
bathroom with piss and blood

onto the street Consciousness has to be some weird

cipher forget it

throw it in a tote bag

Tupperware full of Post-it notes
filing cabinet full of shoes envelope

full of condoms shopping bag full
of shopping bags

Monica Vitti whispers *non lo so non lo so non lo so*

facing Rome's sprawl in 1962
which is still true but it's not a glamorous poem

no longer even
one about love

failed romance becomes a pretext to talk

about alienation attempted or dashed hello's
inside rumpled and damp bedrooms across

great metropolises the lease is buried in pieces O unreal city / any city

under the paving stones our letters
between dry wall under the floor
boards the unknown

to pretend-own

cubic feet

when no one here owns their own excrement rent
-stabilization a means to prevent

self-dispersion across the boroughs, public
green space, self-storage units

three and a half rooms to bracket the civilization

in private we lack

now empty unengaged
to a down and out Dadaist boxer

swept out on a wave / the story gets lost

to the poem when the speaker
begins steadily bleeding compassion for herself

would-be protagonist who were we those people
in room three?

floor slants forty-five degrees

The real collapsing and collapsing
the possible

cascading paint dusts the brow
feeding and feeding a fire of

exquisite unhappiness personal
vanity waterfalls of lost hair unending

chronic lust literature and history
a dust colony / it's the end of the movie

No one gets to be Monica Vitti

just little Cabiria, rough

swept up
in a procession

of teenagers singing

in bright gay party hats
they play accordion
and guitar

for a while she
walks with them

the road at night

●

Like Adorno, I hate everything
about my generation except

we didn't invent jazz,
or anything
not light titanium

faith afloat the digital
ocean on shore Theodore's ghost

and I stand glinting in the sun
lubricated with nostalgia
and bitterness in the Rockaways

the waves will sweep you away

in the Rockaways the waves
sweep children away mix
salt air high-rise penury rising

mysterious uniform mushroom-toned

with the Empire's music blasting
from a Corolla with rims

Jay-Z near Beach 99
chrome and rust tinnitus

grand, impersonal power
personal charisma flexing power

not clothed in that tinny sentiment
love

Songs of self-dissolution
to God

are the only songs

to trust the casual observer notes: The adult tans alone

to be hammered
into salt and sand by the sun
to forget

Well I've heard there's a city
called Glory

I'm just tryin'na
make that city my home

Wade in the water, children

I will row
I will row

toward island someone
else and upon arrival it may slip

away the untruth at the center
of love songs is the stead-

fastness of adoration the truth
of the gospel is
the speaker's dumb wailing and

over there, God, a little
circumspect

●

A few months' personal inertia pooled
here in the waiting room of the state

an officer name-tagged Phil
shudders *I shoulda been a nurse*

after one man accuses him
of acting like he owns this

shit, the waiting room Waiting at some point in
history having liberated

itself from what might happen then everyone leaves
for lunch

and if you do not record
your name

in the log, ma'am
your presence
will not be registered

suspended in time not
registered here

71

suspended in passage through big fake-looking land-

scape, buildings propped up
against the road,

against us, for effect

Space, the defining fact
in a useless body's

rambling
through time

silence in the car silence in my heart / February

large white teddy bears
in cellophane anchor mylar balloons I love you

written in jazzy 80's cursive

across the highway on a dirt mound
the vendor sits

under floodlights
wind
night

watch a table covered in pink and red
carnations bears massed around his legs

crinkle in the cold always here
in the poor neighborhood

on the way to the airport the I love you's

of lovers' potentially lost
or rent hearts not paid
waiting tonight especially

for the possible
transaction

flowers sometimes standing in
for the tensile strength

of the feminine
sometimes for wilting

mutable futures in committed monogamy

further down
God's black house

under flaking white-
wash fallen into splinters

and neat white Baptist
spires every few miles for gallons

on the radio the world
awaits an Arab spring

•

after Osvaldo Lamborghini

Easter Sunday the residents on this stretch
of Alston on card tables and patio chairs watch

two pit bulls pick at a cat
carcass mash it with their faces

on the dividend real liquid southern heat

begins to condense
particles of hyacinth

and bearded iris
collect in the throat

boredom washed over in waves
blurs trees / bends time

boredom is fury intelligence solidarity hunger enunciation

longing kept in check
we pass in front of CHRIST:

NOT NAILS we pass in front of THE MYSTICAL
WORLD a storefront virgin

portable compact merciful pops
from her pink gold conch/halo

magnolias explode late
down the street

filigree the heights crawl
up into their bluest parts

what vegetable stubbornness
carries life up through fissures

(seem to die even as
they begin to bloom)

in the clay earth to live
apart from us pre-historic

supremely disinterested History / the story has stopped

passing through us
it passes through them

what passivity is so vast,
mine, that of the Maltese

who won't go in the yard though
you've paid to have it fenced

who wants their rosy freckled
belly broadcast to pointy blades

●

A landscape passes before you
distractedly many times, may penetrate

the mind after having been a child
for decades he's been a man for weeks

high in the Andes
looking down the rolling

valley of gasoline dust
concrete and recombinant crime

the map will show a mottled record
of population spreading through some

megalopolis in the Americas
between certain decades fading brown

rings around burgundy circles
where bodies live in closest compression

massed together tight draw
new maps with

more mucous / blood mixed
with smog on the brow

when we cross the threshold
to rest / press our faces

into the hard night

unbroken center in the crush
the Cafeteria Romana stately

yellow in its faded modernity soot
darkened awnings peeling flower

-spangled wall-paper the Deco city
center cordoned off

for demolition a wave of political
graffiti a wave of surreal pictures

broken pre-Columbian icons Nazi insignias
sprayed on improbable surfaces Captain

America holds a straw to a huge
pile of blow Gaitán

commemorative mural
murdered in 1948

waving his fists suit taught
over short arms raised

inside a frame so much
smaller than him

square mestizo jaw taught, broken

by history, frame shrunken by same Downtown

swarms with cheap suited lawyer and
secretary colonies in opaque panty-hose

through the crush that delivery
boy rides a motorcycle

in front of the Central Bank
watch the spectators

press their
hard faces tight

into any arid day
distrust sketched

mean against malice

a bride stands
enclosed in her gilt
glass case at the end of the Pasaje Jimenez

flanked by negative space, plus
other mannequin companions
behind, tidy

and proud under dust but shoddy
in comparison to the gem

on the finger / the gangrenous
arm of a dead arcade with watch

and umbrella repair shops
huddled in arches

a man is taping together ruptured
cassette tape long after

five o'clock in 1970 fixing things becomes a form of poverty
of waiting

to preside over a mass
destruction

human density
slicing mountains

there's a story:
progress like desire / destiny inexorable

a heron stands a little
circumspect

embroiders the pond's
edges, then the sky

Here in the heights souls
cleave the haze

the ancestors' immaterial substance
mixed with

cloud laughter

to recognize us as little as we recognize them

massed around knife
pleats of light closer to the sun

gold and purple
acacia / clover

eucalyptus drip

bright mentholated

honey in the oxygen

loose and free inside the lungs

though the meanings of freedom mix and disperse in shallow waters

tadpoles under the finger insects
caught here in insect life

our failure's sameness is pooling in blood
and fiber / flesh / no fidelity

so absolute / some cipher
no one better than the other

we will never have had each other
in the absolute steadfastness of fact

that no one will ever have had
each other is the balm some

essential substance that shrinks from naming from obligation

the nation's wild
flowers bow gently

around our waists
in the open

field bordered by plastic tents that house
the world's carnations

and roses carnivorous, land / water / air
dissolving in

velvet belly for export
invested in wilting mutable futures

we lose our relationship to the land, then we lose
the land

cheeks and foreheads

drink the last rosy
light

●

March's rotting shallows
pool inside my damp parka

a milk carton floats
in a recess by the tracks sunny-side

up against the infinitely
fucked infinitely lucky Phila stars

singed they dimly beat
against the night / my chest

I change / becoming who I've
always been all things happen in time

watch you disappear
into the poetic
adolescent sublime

glint then fade, a gem in Blue Jersey's
pale brown hair

hear in passing women's dreams,
especially

plagued by interrupted intimacy, a second
cast off by the psyche

and I'm tumbling
back

a man walks naked in the morning
down Market huge dick flopping

against his thigh, thing seen
in the panorama
of goodbye

in cold morning with wet face
the senses disperse and mix

after three eclipses dissolve
all certainty I won't

brush my teeth they'll stain with
wine dark feeling

an express bolts through five
commuter towns at a time

each station a bank of sunlight
at five thirty go right through its
petrified goldenness

Springtime's diffidence comes
as no surprise a Northeast

impenetrable / ungreen
as someone who doesn't give

a shit about me, the romance of my problem
anymore / its permutations

will ride beside me many nights and years
the landscape

of emotion dappled by acid
rain on the window pane / displacement

Robert Smithson says
to Nancy Holt, "You don't know

where it's at. You're just a New
Yorker"

here at home, far from home in
America / at sea, figuratively

Men have appeared naked
in my poems before it's just that

I find male public nudity so vulnerable
amazing Stay up

late enough to hear a
woman speak enthusiastically

about how her new bra doesn't
give her back fat (sometimes standing

in for the feminine abject)
muffled through

blankets a spacious emptiness rises
in the back of the throat

beginning with the off-season
carnival in the parking lot of Shea

rides in the night
are light monsters

rise out of wood mulch lots
flecked with cigarette butts

stand at the base of the centrifuge
with Melissa's father a prison guard at Riker's
waiting

to use the twenty mom gave
me to buy a Mets wallet

the spectacle no less appealing for its shabbiness

sends *the boys are back in town*
into the summer arcade

awaits us, full of fake prizes
to tolerate ambiguity
for a long time

to be a true champ
at the crane game

a metal claw
begins to penetrate the outer

edge of the teddy bear's ear / existence
on a pile of other cheap toys

and the fuzzy material
falls limp under its own
loose weight

that you would appear here naked
is vulnerable too,

but no

Memory is crowned in heat and weight / a limpid aura

not the image of

love mercilessly
producing the question of

freedom how will we live
here

in this world not as a sequence of endings
and beginnings

but inside
raw dumb time my dreams are my own

Raleigh/Durham/Chapel Hill Craigslist
is full of four poster beds

tons of area women throwing away
their princess fantasies, mildly surprised

Anna Karenina is
not a self-help book

then, the existence
of the railroad

would announce to our heroine a new world haunts this old one

and the freight cars' passing echoes
through the air conditioner

Titles Available from Subpress:

Bentley, Scott. *The Occasional Tables.*
Bouchard, Daniel. *Diminutive Revolutions.*
Bouchard, Daniel. *Some Mountains Removed.*
Brennan, Sherry. *Of Poems and Their Antecedents.*
Carey, Steve. *Selected Poems.*
Cariaga, Catalina. *Cultural Evidence.*
Carll, Steve, and Bill Marsh. *Tao Drops I Change.*
Davis, Jordan, and Sarah Manguso. (Eds.) *Free Radicals:
American Poets Before Their First Books.*
Dinh, Linh. *All Around What Empties Out.*
Edwards, Kari. *A Day in the Life of P.*
Elliot, Joe. *Opposable Thumbs.*
Evans, Brett. *After School Sessions.*
Fitterman, Robert, and Dirk Rowntree. *War, the Musical.*
Friedlander, Benjamin. *The Missing Occasion of Saying Yes.*
Guthrie, Camille. *In Captivity.*
Guthrie, Camille. *The Master Thief.*
Harrison, Roberto. *Os.*
Hofer, Jen. *Slide Rule.*
Holloway, Rob. *Permit.*
Hull, Jeff. *Spoors.*
Jaramillo, Laura. *Material Girl.*
Lauture, Denize. *The Black Warrior and Other Poems.*
Lenhart, Gary. *Another Look: Selected Prose.*
Lyons, Kimberly. *The Practice of Residue.*
Malmude, Steve. *The Bundle: Selected Poems.*
McNally, John. *Exes for Eyes*
Moxley, Jennifer. *The Middle Room: A Memoir.*
Nguyen, Hoa. *Your Ancient See Through.*
Peters, Mark. *Ooh-La-La-La-Ouch.*
Richards, Deborah. *Last One Out.*
Rothschild, Douglas. *Theogony.*
Sharma, Prageeta. *Bliss to Fill.*
Sinavaina-Gabbard, Caroline. *Alchemies of Distance.*
Stevens, James Thomas, & Caroline Sinavaiana. *Mohawk / Samoa:
Transmigrations.*
Torres, Edwin. *Fractured Humorous.*
Wilkinson, John. *Oort's Cloud.*
Winter, Max. *Walking Among Them.*